The Ghosts of Us

Also by **D. Michael Hardy**:

Pain & Longing: Poetry and Photography

The Ghosts of Us

Poetry

D. Michael Hardy

Clandestine Publishing, LLC

THE GHOSTS OF US Copyright © 2022 D. Michael Hardy. All rights reserved.

Printed in the United States of America. No part of this book may be used or reproduced in any manner whatsoever without written permission from the publisher, except in the case of brief quotations embodied in critical articles and reviews.

For information, contact Clandestine Publishing at:
clandestinepublishing@gmail.com

Clandestine Publishing, LLC
www.clandestinepublishing.com

Cover artwork: Andrii Husak. Used with permission.

Library of Congress Control Number: 2022943522

First paperback edition

ISBN: 979-8-9866394-0-6

For my parents, Ray and Darliene,
whose unconditional love and support have meant everything.

Author's Note

Many of the poems in this book were written during a very dark period in my life, and like always, I use poetry to express those emotions so that I can move forward. Thankfully, they no longer reflect my current state of mind and heart, and while I hope you can understand my thoughts and feelings at the time through the words on these pages, at least on some level, I truly hope you are not also locked in a similar state of darkness and despair as I was. If you are, know that despite what you may think, there is always someone who would rather sit and listen to your story than to your eulogy, and that tomorrow is another day to turn things around. And, if nothing else, you have yourself. You are a beautiful, wonderful, unique human being, and *you* are all you need to survive and thrive, if only you choose to believe in yourself. You are stronger than you know, so keep going, keep fighting. If you feel you can't find anyone who will listen, call this number, and they will:

National Suicide Prevention Lifeline
1-800-273-8255

Your story isn't over

;

"Poetry is what happens when nothing else can."
– Charles Bukowski

The Ghosts of Us

The Ghosts of Us*

Our shadows
still walk
these streets.

Like ghosts,
they haunt
our every
move.

*This poem was originally published in my first book, *Pain & Longing: Poetry and Photography*. It became the inspiration for the book you now hold in your hands. *The Ghosts of Us* is a reflection on the past; on the people, places, and experiences that made me who I am today, and I hope that you find comfort and solace in the words I have left on these pages.

D. Michael Hardy

Immortality

When I'm gone,
don't bury me
beneath a marble plaque
to gaze down upon,
don't honor me
with a fine stone bench
to rest and reflect
on days past,
or plant me
as a tree
to bloom but once a year,
remember me only
through the words
I've left on the page,
through the memories
we've shared over drinks,
over dinner or long drives
or brief encounters
or vacations
to beautiful places,
keep me alive
by speaking of me often,
so that in these small ways
perhaps
I'll live forever.

Remnants

We hold onto
remnants of the past
to remind us
how horrible
we once were,
or how beautiful,
and sometimes,
the ghosts of the past
refuse
to remain silent.

D. Michael Hardy

Nana

You were a ghost
since birth,
a figment
of a grandmother
left only to dreams
and mothering fantasies.

What might it have been like
to be held in your embrace?
To have been spoiled
by your loving grace?

I'll never know,
and that's a loss
both of us
were forced
to endure.

Must We

Must we continue
as if nothing
ever happened?

I know
the world goes on
but
I'd just like to
step out of it
for a little while,
just leave me be
in my solitude
to mourn,
to remember,
while the rest of you
carry on
as if this most
horrible thing
never happened.

Other Plans

This old
jaded heart
still wants to
love,
but the whole
world
seems to have
other plans
in mind.

Never Again

Today,
I woke in time
to watch the sunrise,
sat out on my patio
sipping coffee
as the early birds
got their worms,
the squirrels flicking
their angry little tails at them,
sunlight streaming
through bare tree branches,
casting tall shadows across
dead grass and blooming Aloe plants.

Then I napped
through another
miserably hot afternoon,
rose from bed just in time
to catch the sunset,
a glass of red
in hand,
those damned birds
and squirrels
still moving about,
though not as lively
as they'd been
in the morning.

I watched the moon

D. Michael Hardy

replace the sun,
holding court
with the stars,
and together we drank
and danced
and laughed
and wrote
until that golden goddess
rose again,
and I knew it was time
to retire.

I slipped
beneath the sheets,
one cat
atop my pillow,
another at my feet
and knew – the day
had been a damned good one,
and it would never
come again.

The Pull

I felt the pull
today,
those jagged claws
tugging at my back,
and it was all
I could do
to hold on,
to refuse
to give in,
to keep myself
from falling back
into that darkness,
a darkness
I know so well,
a darkness
that may one day
pull me down
for
the
last
time.

D. Michael Hardy

A Moment

And it's okay
if you need
some time
to yourself,
we all need a moment
of peace,
to think and reflect,
to plan and plot,
somewhere alone
in a place we find
most beautiful,
in a place we feel
most at home
in this too often
cruel world
of chaos and cutthroats.

Make Believe

Everything is pale and gray,
ashes
everywhere I turn.

This ground and sky
blur together so perfectly
it's impossible to tell
what's up and who's down,
impossible to tell
darkness from daylight.

We are,
all of us,
doomed
without even realizing it.

Hope is dead,
and I
am but a figment
of your inebriated imagination.

Have another drink
and make believe
I'm still here.

D. Michael Hardy

Where Sadness Begins

I am buried in books.

I am drowning in liquor
and loneliness,
a solitary prison cell
I've constructed
for myself.

There is no
love, no
intimacy
other than
my own.

This
is where
sadness
begins.

Tomorrow

Another day gone
and I've barely
accomplished
all I set out to do,
squandered my time
on frivolous activities,
I keep telling myself
tomorrow's
another day,
and tomorrow
I'll write those 1000 words,
tomorrow
I'll make those phone calls
I've been putting off,
tomorrow
I'll clean the car
and trim the night-blooming jasmine
and fix the toilet,
tomorrow
I'll clean out the shed
and rake the yard
and send out
a few more stories,
and maybe I'll even
lift those weights
collecting dust in the corner.

I'll get to it all
tomorrow,

D. Michael Hardy

be a better version of myself,
learn a new language,
learn to play guitar,
meditate in the garden.

Because tomorrow
is another day,
another chance
to turn it all around,
to learn from our mistakes,
to tell someone
you love them,
to ask forgiveness
for all the wrongs
done to others.

Tomorrow
is another day,
until it isn't.

Two Fundamental Things

I'm of the age now
where lately
I've been thinking a lot
about mortality,
about what compels us
to keep going
despite the odds,
about why so many of us
feel the need to leave
a mark behind,
and I wonder
how much longer I have left
to make my own.

I can say
for the most part
I've enjoyed my life,
but it's missing
two fundamental things
that I hope to attain
before its inevitable conclusion:
a literary canon,
and a long-lasting love
of my life.
I'm working on the former,
but the latter
continues to elude me.

D. Michael Hardy

Settle

Perhaps
in death
we can learn
to agree
on the things
we could not
settle
in life.

Twenty Years Since

Twenty years since
and I find myself wondering
what you might
look like now,
how much your laugh
might have changed,
if you'd still love
Brandon Lee
as much
as you did then,
if you'd be married,
single, happy,
in love, solitary,
a famous writer
like Anne Rice,
but most of all
I wonder
how things would be
between us now,
if we'd still be
best friends,
estranged,
or something
more akin
to brother and sister.

You were never defined,
a dear friend, a sister
I never had,
but your love
was never questioned,
and I'll spend

D. Michael Hardy

the rest of my days
loving you, missing you,
wondering
what might have become
of us
twenty years since.

I Run

When I find myself
    losing control,
        I run.

    When the darkness
        seeps in through the cracks
            like smoke,
                I run.

    When the days
        drag on
            like a body,
                I run.

When the sadness
    floods my eyes
        and heart
            and lungs,
                I run.

And when I'm certain
    I can't go on
        any longer,
and the barrel of a gun
        laughs at me
            from the dresser drawer,
                      I run.

    I run
        to escape the demons
            that live inside
                this terrible mind

D. Michael Hardy

      of mine,
           and so far,
                it's working.

           And so,
                I run.

In Isolation

It's a Friday night
and I'm getting drunk,
alone,
because there's little else to do
on a Friday night
in isolation
when you're over
watching movies
and reading books
and playing darts
and talking to your cats (which never ends)
and I'm at that point
of breaking isolation rules
and hosting a party
because what is life
without social interaction?
Sure, solitude
is beautiful,
but it can also
be maddening
and I find myself
moving into that zone
of individualism
that leads to either insanity
or suicide
and wanting a more human contact
than I've had in these past
six months.

D. Michael Hardy

The Past

Don't
erase the past.

Use it.

Then go out
and create a future
you'd be proud
to teach
your grandchildren about.

Doom and Gloom

People often
misunderstand me,
I'm not all doom
and gloom,
I have days
where I laugh
so hard it hurts,
days where I love
to go out
with my girl
on some wild
adventure
in the city
or on the beach,
days where I speak
to my cats
in some silly voice
as if they're infants
while rubbing
their fat bellies,
days I cherish
sitting around a fire
or game of cards
with good friends
and strong libations,
and I have days,
though rare,
where I still hold out
hope

D. Michael Hardy

that the human race
will find a way back
to its humanity,
and save itself
from our collective
doom and gloom.

Baby Bats

So many faces
have come and gone
on that old
battered dance floor
in Ybor,
drifting
between that infinite
darkness
and those spectacular
pulsing lights,
the fog flowing
like a specter
all around us
and the cigarette smoke
that seemed endless
yet ephemeral.

I've known
so many souls
and lost them as well,
lost to time,
or distance,
or death,
or broken relationships,
or simply due to
a
lack
of
human

D. Michael Hardy

effort
on both sides,
but
whenever I've gone back
to that old castle
in the city,
their faces
have been replaced
by new faces,
younger and more
hopeful
than mine,
and I can't help
but wonder
what has become
of us
and those good
old days
when we were
nothing more than
baby bats,
eager
for that favorite song
to play,
and for our turn
on the dance floor.

Things We Love the Most

It's difficult
to keep things looking
nice, shiny and new,
they get worn, scarred,
scraped and bruised,
they get dented
and burnt,
faded and rusted,
tattered and torn.

And I often wonder
which is loved more?

That thing on the shelf,
kept safely behind glass,
not a scratch, smudge,
or scar in sight?

Or is it that thing
beaten up,
held together by string
and duct tape,
hope and good intentions,
looking to all the world
like it's been dragged
through Hell?

D. Michael Hardy

How Little I Remember

of our last day
together,
our final moments,
your mother called,
told me
you're in the hospital,
dying,
come say goodbye,
hurry,
and I collapsed
on my living room floor,
devastated, trembling,
this was the end,
and nothing I could do
would ever change that.

I reached for the bottle,
it wasn't even noon yet,
and the rest of that day
drifts
in swirling memories,
from that phone call
in my living room,
to that cold,
sterile hospital room
where I held your hand
for the last time,
from that old dive bar
where I got stinking drunk,

The Ghosts of Us

to my twilight bedroom
where I cried
myself to sleep.

I did my best
to drown it all out.

How little I remember,
but oh, how I'll never
forget.

D. Michael Hardy

Brothers

I still recall
those long-lost days
of youth,
the two of us
playing, carefree
on the rickety swing set
beneath orange-leaf oaks,
or sliding down the stairs
on magic carpets
in that big house
in Maryland,
those crazy neighbor kids
egging us on,
laughing to tears
as we tumbled.

And those white winter days
sledding down
that terrifying hill,
defying death
all the way,
sometimes happy,
sometimes fighting,
but always family,
always brothers,
and that's one thing
that will never change.

I'm sure I might have

annoyed you at times,
and we may not have always
been as close
as we could've been,
yet,
as we've gotten older
I've come to appreciate
and respect
your opinions and views
on politics and life,
your talented written musings
on everything from
that Christmas our father
played the neighborhood Santa,
to your ten-hour drive
to New Orleans for brunch,
but most of all,
for your unwavering dedication
on an entirely new
way of life.

D. Michael Hardy

Drunken God

Some nights
I tell myself
"I'm not gonna get drunk,
I'll just have one or two,"
then convince myself
a third is needed
to even myself out,
and before long
I'm pouring a fifth
or sixth glass,
the music's blasting
and the neighbors
have called the cops,
and in the afternoon
I wake up
with a crushing hangover,
my clothes strewn
all over the room,
and try to remember
at what point
I slipped from
being human
and turned into
that old drunken god.

Memories of My Grandfather

The older I get,
the more
memories of my grandfather
recede into oblivion,
and I try
in futility
to hold onto them,
but the sound of his voice,
his laughter,
are now gone,
a chasm
my mind can no longer
penetrate,
and yet some things remain,
like the scent
of cigars
and fresh cut wood,
big bear hugs
and butterfingers
and apple sauce,
that warm, toothless grin
that would often greet me
after school,
the old station wagon
with wood paneling
and red seats,
the black-framed eyeglasses
and pocket knife
always at the ready,

D. Michael Hardy

and then
those dark green oxygen tanks
that kept him alive
in that final year,
the year he taught me
what it truly meant
to die.

Shadow

I am merely
a shadow
of my former self,
living out
the echoes
of a life
that has lost
any meaning
long ago.

D. Michael Hardy

Endure

There are so many
moments
now, when I wish
I could just call you up
and talk about nothing,
just hear your voice
on the phone,
your laugh or those things
you'd always say
about guns
about women
about Mustangs,
so many moments
I wish I could just stop by
and visit,
but the tragedy of living
is that you eventually outlive
those you love,
and you learn
just how hard it is
to live without them,
to miss the sound of their voice,
their scent or mannerisms,
their quirks and their crazy drama,
and you wonder,
how much more must I endure?

How many more funerals
must I attend?

The Ghosts of Us

One is too many,
and yet we endure,
in the hope
that we are still able
to find beauty
in life after the loss.

And you know what?

We do.

D. Michael Hardy

Unanchored

I find I am running
out of reasons to stay
alive,
the joys I once
cherished
do little these days
to keep my heart
afloat,
I'm just drifting along,
unanchored
in a roiling sea,
and little by little
I feel the water
seeping in,
and I can't seem
to remember
if I ever
learned to swim.

Monsters are Real

For a child
once terrified
of the dark,
of the monsters
lurking under his bed
and in closets,
I've grown up
to become
accustomed to it,
thriving even,
in the candlelight
and shadows,
and yet,
I continue to be
appalled
at the horrors
committed daily
by the real monsters,
the ones
who call themselves
human.

D. Michael Hardy

Beyond Sleep

And the minute
I lay head to pillow
I know
I'll pass out,
but it's those images
which lay
beyond sleep
that I fear most,
that I do not wish
to see tonight,
not again,
not in the state
I'm in,
not in the state
of this world
as it is,
and so I keep myself
company,
with a little help
from Mr. Jim Beam,
doing my best
to keep those
particular demons at bay,
to keep a semblance
of my sanity,
to remember those days
before my world
changed forever.

The Ghosts of Us

As if
I could ever
forget.

And yet,
that is what I fear
most of all.

D. Michael Hardy

Nothing More Than

When we were
young
we took life
for granted,
wondering
what it would be like
once we're older,
or old,
hobbling along
with canes in hand,
our hair
gray or gone,
laughing
as our bodies
faded to dust.

But I often
wondered,
what if I didn't make it?
What if you came out
one morning,
thirty years later,
walked into the living room,
hair disheveled,
coffee or tea in hand,
only to see
my ghost,
the chair
I'd often be found in

as I drank my morning joe
and read a book
empty,
with only the impression
of me
left in my wake?

Did I make it
to be that old man
I used to write about?
Or am I nothing more
than a gust of wind,
a distant memory,
a name on the lips
of those who knew me,
rarely spoken
but thought of often?

I only hope
I am not
forgotten.

D. Michael Hardy

Father

Father,
I wonder,
are you proud
that your son
is a struggling writer
rather than a successful lawyer,
college professor,
maybe even a pastor
at the local church?
I've followed
my own path,
working the words
every day,
although often slower
than either of us
would prefer.

Father,
I hope
you know
I've always respected
you, and the path
you chose
to support us all,
the sacrifices
you endured,
the wisdom
you bestowed
over the years,

The Ghosts of Us

the honesty
and integrity
of your words,
all honorable things
which I try
to live up to.

Father,
I wish
we had another
forty years
to do it all over again,
the Christmases and
vacations,
the laughter
and even the arguments too,
but all I can do
now, is write faster,
hug harder,
visit more often,
and hope
that it's enough
in the end.

D. Michael Hardy

Lament

Whatever happened
to those poets
who'd write poems
pages long,
poets
like Bukowski,
like Kerouac,
like Ginsberg and Frost and Keats
and so many before them?

Those guys knew
what it took
to bare the soul,
to lay down and split their chests
wide open
for all the world
to see.

Nowadays,
Too many poets
write a line
or two
and call that poetry.

I call it
a fucking slogan,
but hell,
who am I
to judge?

The Ghosts of Us

I'm just as guilty
as the rest of them.

Half of my poems
don't ever make it
to page two.

And even then,
who knows
if they're any good.

D. Michael Hardy

A Romantic Poem

I don't typically write
romantic poetry,
that just isn't my style,
but I admire those poets
who can write about
love, passion,
matters of the heart
so eloquently
it's as if they'd just
split open a vein,
poured their love out
in thin red rivulets,
or vomited it up
in chunks
on the carpet
at their lover's feet,
only to be rejected
by shallow souls
in favor of
the dashing doctor,
the bull-headed banker,
the corporate connoisseur,
anyone
whose bank account
hits over five figures,
because love
always seems easier
when money
isn't a problem.

And how's that
for romantic?

D. Michael Hardy

Fresh

I want to keep
this pain
fresh,
I don't want it to
heal.

Like a cut
scabbed over,
I want to keep
picking
until it bleeds,
again and again.

I don't want
to just see the fading
scar,
but the blood
mixing with tears
falling,
 falling.

That Night in December

I didn't want to disclose
what happened
that night in December,
for fear
I couldn't handle
the disappointment
I knew would swell
in your eyes,
and since then
I've been dealing
with the aftermath
of that decision,
carrying the weight of it
just beneath the surface,
my smiles a mask
I've been forced to wear
for every dinner,
every holiday
and evening conversation,
and I hope this poem
is as far as I'll ever go
to full disclosure
of what happened
that night in December.

D. Michael Hardy

Second Thought

I sat there
for a long while
in the cold
porcelain tub,
staring
at the soap scum
on the tiled walls
by candlelight,
cradling that 357
like a baby,
my one-way ticket
into oblivion,
those dark thoughts
flexing their muscles
yet again,
but then I thought
of you, my dear,
how wearisome
it might be
to live
with my dissatisfied
ghost,
shuffling about
at all hours,
rustling book pages
in the library
and chasing the cats
at 3am,
keeping you up

when all you wanted
was to dream
of a life
where I'd made
better choices,
a life in which
the two of us
still drove to see
sunsets
over the ocean,
still ventured
into the city
to see our friends,
still soaked
in warm waters
as we gazed
at the stars,
and so I crawled
out of that tub,
tucked that baby
back into bed,
drank a shot
of whiskey
with the moon,
and congratulated myself
on another day
victorious.

D. Michael Hardy

Never Assume

You always assume
you have more time,
more time to catch up,
to get together,
to reminisce,
to make plans,
until you don't.

And then all you can do
is hold on to those memories
as tight as you can
for as long as you can
and hope
they don't fade
from memory.

Genius Bullshit

Over the past few days
I've written
about a dozen poems
while drunk
on whiskey and life,
and maybe
they're bullshit,
or maybe
they're genius,
it's hard to say
what one person will like
and another will hate
these days,
but I try
not to concern
myself
with things
I can't control.

D. Michael Hardy

Reminder

Sometimes
it takes a tragedy
to remind us
just how beautiful
life can be.

Charles

I never really knew you,
old man,
too preoccupied
with your sports,
or news,
or whatever the hell else
you chose the tv
over us,
your grandkids, for,
but I'll never forget
the scent of that pipe
you loved so much,
perched
on the side table,
a companion
to your ratty old recliner
that got more attention
than any one of us,
but I never took it personally,
I knew
you'd had your days
of hell
on this earth,
and those nights
spent
in front of that
old Panasonic
were the only times
since the birth

D. Michael Hardy

of your sixth
and final son
you'd had to yourself
in over forty years.

Tragedy

The saddest thing
I think a writer
can do
is pretend
as if the past
never happened,
because the past
makes for some
damned-good
plotlines.

D. Michael Hardy

All Those Moments

We were all
so young,
full of teen angst
and rebellion,
confusion,
passion,
rage and hope
for the future,
a future that was wide open
like a gaping wound,
and we had no idea
how we'd fair
in the world at large,
whether we'd be
successful in our ventures
or failures,
whether we'd catch
those dreams
that kept eluding us
or become our parents,
but we were so eager
to find out
we sometimes failed
to pause
and appreciate
what was right in front
of us:
a beautiful day,
splendid company,

The Ghosts of Us

laughter, innocence,
tender kisses,
a good book
on a rainy day,
music
that moved us
to tears,
all those moments
worth living for.

D. Michael Hardy

Hollywood Vampire

Those days
living
in Hollywood,
working odd jobs
just to barely
pay the bills,
going out
to the clubs
every night,
veiled in makeup
and myth,
a vampire
in a city
of broken angels,
praying
for prey,
flirting
with darkness
and death,
now feel like
a dream,
a montage
of thoughts and images,
splices of film
left
on the cutting room floor,
bruised
and blood-splattered,
left

to make a new movie,
one I now build
with words,
with tears and blood,
with those memories
purloined
from a thousand
sordid nights,
each one sacred,
telling me secrets
the world
should never know.

And yet
they will,
under the guise
of fiction,
because secrets
never remain secret
forever.

D. Michael Hardy

The Way It Goes Down

This is the way
it goes down.

All I've known
and all I've become,
you took in hand
and tore apart,
and this gentle flesh
you just couldn't resist.

Save me,
I have no hope,
take me away
to live another lie.

The scars are still here
to remind me
of all the pain,
and pleasures inflicted.

And here I find,
I find myself alone,
wandering in darkness,
no place to call home.

Save me,
I have no soul,
now that it's over
I don't wanna die.

So this is the way
it goes down.

The Ghosts of Us

Try to hold on
to a nameless frame,
when all I've done
and all I've tried
has only taken me
to the ends of your lies.

And all I know
no longer believes
in me,
And all I believe
is no longer known
to me.

D. Michael Hardy

The Storm

Much like a storm,
depression
passes slowly,
a thief
in the night,
robbing us
of our
ability to see
clearly
all the things
that could save us
from otherwise
certain doom.

We must hold strong,
wait it out,
allow it
to pass
over us,
endure
the rain,
the dark clouds,
the harsh lightning
strikes in our minds,
the collapsing trees
and broken windows,
so when the sun
eventually rises,
despite the damage

The Ghosts of Us

that's been done,
we can rise up
once again,
our walls beaten,
but our foundations
still standing.

D. Michael Hardy

Laceration

When asked
about writing,
Bukowski once said,
"Don't try
unless it comes
pouring out of you,"
but I disagree,
sometimes
the words
trickle out
like blood
from a minor wound,
but when they do,
they can be just as brilliant
as a profoundly deep
laceration.

Ghosted

There's damage
that's been done,
an upending
of roots,
the soil's
turned cold,
and I'm flailing
against these final
winter winds,
left wondering
where you've gone,
and why
you won't answer
my calls.

D. Michael Hardy

Your Legacy

For all the years
I sought your advice,
for all the times
you helped me up
when I was down,
or lost,
or penniless,
I just want to say
"Thank you."

But thank you
doesn't quite do it justice,
does it?

You gave me far more
than I expected
or deserved.
You had the courage
to say "no"
when you knew my ideas
were flawed
or simply no good for me.

You taught me
the value of morality,
of managing my money
and understanding the importance
of paying bills first
and having fun later,

responsibility before recreation,
of always striving
to tell the truth,
even when it's not
what people want to hear,
and of understanding the value
of integrity.

For all of these things
I can never repay you,
except with my undying
gratitude
and the promise
that I'll do my best
to keep your legacy
alive.

D. Michael Hardy

A Fighting Chance

Life
has its ways
of pulling you
down
or lifting you
up,
but
so long as you
keep going,
keep fighting
for what you
believe in,
keep striving
to be better
today
than you were
yesterday,
you just might
stand
a fighting chance
to become
something beautiful,
something you've always
dreamt of becoming.

So keep fighting.

Ticking

I have much work to do,
I need to get
busy,
I know, the clock is
ticking,
ticking,
ticking,
much like the clock
inside the heart
of a bomb,
and if I don't finish
when the clock runs out
at least know
I tried,
I tried,
I tried.

I hope
you
can say
the same
when your clock
stops ticking
too.

D. Michael Hardy

Less Than

I'll never forget
the first time
I read Ellis,
such a short book
but I was transfixed
by the voice, the style,
the desolation and depravity
of those kids,
zombies,
wandering
through the bleak streets
of 1980s Los Angeles.

I must've read that book
a couple dozen times at least,
and then there were
the others too,
the Rules and the Psycho,
and they're what led me
to living
in the city of angels
in search of myself,
and with the desire,
conviction, ego
and guts
to finally
take myself seriously
as a writer.

Circling

My mind
keeps circling the drain
of your final
moments,
desperate
for answers,
for a way back
in time,
for a way to
save you
from yourself.

What were you thinking
on that last
day,
in your final hours,
minutes,
seconds,
before you chose
to leave us all?

Were you thinking of
your daughter,
who would have to grow up
without her mother?
Or your family,
your friends,
who would spend
a lifetime asking

D. Michael Hardy

the same questions
why, why, why?

Did you have a moment
of doubt?
Were you scared?
Were you excited?
Anxious?
Relieved?
At peace?

I keep asking
all these questions
again, and again
and yet,
no answers surface,
no solace comes,
and so
I keep circling
that drain,
patiently waiting
for the day
that maybe
I'll get to ask you
myself.

My Only Comfort

Tonight
I will drink
myself
to sleep,
my only comfort
residing
in the words
I've left
on the page,
the company
of my feline companions,
and the soothing
numbness
of alcohol.

D. Michael Hardy

Unsatisfied

Crazy
how some people complain when it's
too cold in the winter,
too hot in the summer,
too crowded at Disneyland,
too desolate in a bar
on a Tuesday night,
too loud in night clubs,
too quiet in funeral parlors,
too wet in Seattle,
too dry in Albuquerque.

Crazy
how some people say they
never have enough food to eat,
enough money to spend,
enough books to read,
enough sex,
enough jewelry,
enough socks,
enough time in the day
to eat, shop, read, fuck, sleep.

Crazy
how some people
are always rushing from
here to there,
always cursing their neighbors,
always watching too much television,
always bitching about their weight,
always planning their days,
weeks, months, lives, deaths.

Crazy
how some people
never admit defeat
or when they're wrong,
never follow their dreams,
never try anything just once,
never figure out who they are,
never realize their potential,
their weaknesses, flaws, talents, dreams.

It's crazy,
you know,
how some people
are just never
satisfied
with the things
they have,
the people
who love them,
or their place
in the world.

D. Michael Hardy

Time to Move

Sometimes in life
you need a change,
a change in scenery,
a change in plot,
something that will shake things up
so violently
that the landscape will be
unrecognizable
when the dust settles.

When those times come,
you'll know,
it's time to move,
it's time to grow,
it's time to become
someone else,
someone
you were always
meant to be.

So move.

Learn to Fly

These ghosts
that haunt us,
that we carry
on our shoulders,
are a burden
we can no longer
afford to bear.

We must learn
to let them go,
slip them
from our souls,
bury them
in the past,
where they can no longer
do us harm.

Only then
can we finally
learn to fly.

D. Michael Hardy

Face The Music

Face the music
was all she said
when she looked at me,
eyes so full of gloom,
sweet but dirty,
razorblade lips,
the suitcase full of smiles
and rented heart spaces,
hollowed out holes
failing to fulfill
the faith I had
in you.

She said with shame,
a voice so full of pain,
"this is not the same,"
and her smile is a cut
with horror-show lipstick,
there's scars on my eyes,
the fist-throwing lies,
bruise-body covered,
and I'm just a mannequin
in your world.

I'm tragedy born
with pages torn
from my ribs,
and the heart is a
mechanical toy,
erratically pulsing
with batteries dying.

The Ghosts of Us

Don't give a fuck
'cause I'm not really me,
broken finger trigger
has blown the head off,
blood-soaked despair,
this time wasted.

Face the music,
that's what it comes down to
in the end.

Face the music,
'cause they said you can never
go home again.

D. Michael Hardy

The Bottle or the Bullet

I tried
to give it up,
the alcohol,
but found everything
so goddamned boring
I could barely stand it.

And I wondered
why was I bothering?
Why torture myself
with this mundane life?

It was either
the bottle or the bullet,
that voice kept insisting,
so I take another drink
and the world opens up
like a flower,
or a bomb,
I'm never quite sure which.

Over This

I no longer wished
to work those
numbers,
or watch those
lists,
I grew tired
of the endless phone calls,
the bullshit requests.

All I wanted
was to write,
to be surrounded by
books
and words
and positive energy,
to create
something beautiful,
something real,
something that would last
far longer than your
greedy enterprise,
and something
that would bring me
more satisfaction
than that eight to five Hell
I kept on living.

D. Michael Hardy

Keep Going

I can lament
the past
or wonder about
the future,
and although
I miss certain people
dearly
whom I know I'll never see again
in this life,
or whose path
no longer aligns with
my own,
I can at least say
that I'm grateful
to still be breathing,
to still be making memories
and petting my cats
and reading the good books,
to still taste the good foods
and drink the fine wines,
to still be able
to love,
to laugh,
to learn
new things every day.

This life is both beautiful
and cruel
but it is always

what we choose to make it,
so long as we keep going.

And so
we keep going
one day
at a time.

D. Michael Hardy

Apparition

Dust
covers everything
around me.

It clings
to the walls,
to the books
on shelves
left untouched
by curious hands,
it spins and swirls
in late afternoon
sunbeams,
coalescing
in corners
oft forgotten,
and I imagine
it's your apparition
come back
to dance with me
one
last
time.

Santa Monica Boulevard

I often tell people
when I think fondly
of my time living in
Los Angeles,
"I once puked
on Santa Monica Boulevard!"
And sure, maybe
it's not something
to be proud of,
but it's a moment
I'll never forget,
nor will the woman
on the corner
who watched
as I hung out my driver door
clutching the wheel
and spewed my soul,
hot and vicious,
all over that road
made famous
by song and film,
then drove off
into that rising
golden sun,
a perfect ending
to another Hollywood
tale.

D. Michael Hardy

Never Give Up (on Your Dreams)

I stopped talking
about my dreams,
about those impossible realities
when it felt as if
there was no longer
anyone
who wanted to listen
to my ridiculous
fantasy ramblings.

I kept them hidden,
as coveted as heirlooms,
working on them
in silence,
in solitude,
in a purgatory
I'd designed,
all my own,
until the day
those dreams
finally
became a reality.

And then I was free
to talk about them
once more.

Not a Poet

I'm not really
a poet,
I'll admit,
poems come to me
as infrequently
as dreams,
or checks in the mail,
rarely and without
notice,
but always
a welcome surprise.

D. Michael Hardy

Hopefully Proud

When I was a little boy
you'd take me shopping,
our Saturday afternoons together,
and I'd suffer through
the agony of clothes
and shoes and sometimes hardware
just to get to the toy store,
the comic book shop,
maybe the movies,
and often times you'd reward me
with a new toy
if I was good and patient
the whole time, especially
at the doctor's office,
even though
I rarely ever was.

I haven't forgotten
all you've done
for all of us, not just me,
how much you've suffered
and sacrificed
so that the rest of us
could be happy, content,
our bellies full
from all those countless meals
you slaved over
night and day.

The words "thank you"
don't even come close
to expressing the gratitude,
the appreciation
for all you've done
and all you continue to do
for me.

You've helped me grow
into the man I've become,
full of dreams and ideas,
hopes and yes, fears too,
and what I hope most of all
is that I'm a man
you can be proud to call
your son.

D. Michael Hardy

Carpe Diem

I woke
to news of your death,
and it was just
another reminder
that this life
is but a flash,
a gift
we must seize
and cherish
every day,
and that none of us
know
just how long
we have
to laugh with friends,
to kiss those we love,
and to make our mark
before the reaper
comes knocking.

Devoured

We're all flawed
imperfect souls
searching for balance,
searching for connection
in a world
that values
materialism over charity,
conformity over individualism,
obedience over free will,
and the truth is
these values
are killing us,
eating our souls
from the inside out,
and yet most of us
close our eyes
and smile
as we're slowly
and irrevocably
devoured.

D. Michael Hardy

Old Black Guitar

This old black guitar
resting silently
in the corner
collecting dust,
I keep telling myself
I'll rescue it,
tune it up, learn to play,
not professionally,
those rock star dreams
are long gone,
but for pleasure,
a hobby
I can tell others about,
maybe play a few songs
when friends come over
for cards and drinks,
sing a few lines
of Pink Floyd or Nirvana,
The Cure or Bowie,
but that old black guitar
just keeps sitting there,
watching me, mocking me,
somehow knowing
we'll never touch each other
ever again
until the garage sale
next spring.

A Childhood Regret

I was half-asleep,
twelve or so,
when my mother
cracked open my door
in the middle
of the night
to whisper,
"Granddaddy died,"
and I remember saying,
"Okay,"
and slipping back
into unconsciousness,
eager to discover
where my dreams might lead,
only later to realize
how cold and uncaring
that must've seemed
to her, my mother,
who'd just lost
the only other man
aside my father
who'd promised
to love her
forever.

D. Michael Hardy

No Warning Signs

One day
it will happen
when you're least
prepared,
and it'll hit
like a punch
to the gut,
there'll be no
conversations,
no warning signs
you could've missed,
only the blood spatter
on the wall,
the empty hole
of head and heart,
the flashing lights
in the dead of night,
the unanswered questions
of why, why, why,
and that void of
consciousness
that will haunt
every waking moment
left spent not busy
with the trivialities
and distractions of life.

This World

This world
is so often
too much
and not enough
all at once.

It is constantly
testing us,
pushing us
beyond our measure,
and not all of us
pass the final.

D. Michael Hardy

These Damned Poems

These past few nights
I've stayed up
well past sunrise
listening to jazz
or blues or darkwave,
drinking whiskey or wine,
and I know I shouldn't
because I've got responsibilities,
work and chores
and daylight duties,
but every night
I stay awake,
I keep writing
these damned poems,
so I guess
it's justified.

Pants Down

I've no memory
of the moment
this darkness
worked its way
into my brain,
I feel it's been there
ever since the womb,
and you'd think
I'd have found a way
to defeat its potent
malignancy
after all these years,
that I would've
found a way
to beat this fucker down,
get up and live my life
like some normal person,
eat cereal, drink coffee,
go to work
with a smile plastered
on my face,
but its presence
always catches me,
pants down,
deer in headlights,
and it takes
everything I have,
every ounce of strength
and focus

D. Michael Hardy

and desire
that's left in me
just to lift the pen,
or get out of bed,
or make believe
that I'm doing alright,
when I am anything but.

Nostalgia

Nostalgia
is that thing
which keeps us
looking in the rearview,
hoping
that stray dog
makes it
across traffic,
when instead,
we should be
paying attention
to the road
ahead of us.

D. Michael Hardy

Those Days

I sometimes miss
those long-lost days
living
off the unemployment checks,
spending early afternoons
writing
in that café down the street,
driving
northeast on the freeway,
windows down, wind in my face,
to meet my girl for lunch,
and afterwards,
browsing
the bookstore aisles
till sunset.

In those days,
before the eight-hour time-killer,
the coffee tasted richer,
the food more satisfying,
the words flowed more freely,
but those books
remained my constant saviors,
keeping me sane
in a world of lunatics,
reminding me
there are far greater things
than dealing
with the bullshit
of mediocre people.

Begin Again

Start over,
begin again,
wash your hands
of the things
that no longer
serve you,
love you,
attend to you,
comfort you
or elevate you.

You deserve it.

Even if
you refuse
to admit it.

D. Michael Hardy

Dangerous Ground

When the lines of the fiction
you're writing
and the reality
you're living
suddenly become so
skewed
you begin to think
what your protagonist
would do
rather than what you
would do,
you know you're treading
on dangerous ground.

Echoes

There still remain
echoes
of us
on those moonlit
sandy beaches,
our first late night
rendezvous
under the stars,
two strangers
yet with so much
in common,
who found each other
later in life
than expected,
although maybe
just in time,
and if you listen
closely,
on nights when the moon
is full
and the sky is lit up
by a million stars,
you can still hear
our laughter
as it echoes
on the waves
crashing
along the shoreline.

D. Michael Hardy

My Own Devices

Left alone
to my own devices
and I'll kill
every fucking
bottle
in the room.

Walk Her Streets

There is a subtle longing
whenever I think of
that city now,
her long, sleek towers
kissing the sky,
her curvaceous highways
guiding us into sin,
the ways she always makes you feel
powerless
yet empowered to become more
than your infantile dreams,
and she lingers there,
not quite
in the back
of my mind,
a little closer
than comfort,
the occasional reminders
revealing themselves
in books, in movies,
in memories
that crash like waves
in my dreams,
and I don't want to
forget
all those sordid,
splendid nights,
or the dull, drawn-out days
spent struggling

D. Michael Hardy

to get to them,
but remembering
hurts as much
as it heals,
and I've no idea
how to write about her
without that longing
taking root
and manifesting
into a sublime darkness
that takes days
to recover from.

At least not until I
walk her streets
again
with fresh eyes
and an open heart
and the desire
to let it all go
once and for all.

Continue

So long
as I continue
to speak your name,
my friend,
you will never
be forgotten.

D. Michael Hardy

Most Honest

The other night
I admitted
to my girl
I feel most
human
when I'm drunk,
being sober
makes me feel like
an alien,
and that's the
most honest
I've been with anyone
in a long,
long time.

Hidden

I've been hiding
this darkness
so long
I barely recognize it
anymore.

It's become a part of me –
a tattoo
I've no memory of getting,
a cancer
I'm not yet aware of –
and I've no idea
how to rid myself
of its
persistent
malignance.

D. Michael Hardy

Gone

You slipped away
when I closed my eyes
so suddenly
it was almost as if
you were never really here
at all.

Grateful

I'm grateful
for the gift
of another day
to breathe
and watch the sunset,
to feel the cool breeze
whisper on my face,
to spend another night
on this earth
with my cats
by my side,
to write the right words
and read the great books
and listen to the music
that stirs my soul
so profoundly.

I'm grateful
for having friends and family
who would be there
for me
should I call,
for a woman who loves me
despite my many flaws,
for the conversation
I had tonight,
and the hope of another
tomorrow,
because another tomorrow

D. Michael Hardy

is never promised,
never a guarantee
to any of us.

And in my darkest moments,
I do my best
to remind myself
of these things,
and that beyond every moment
of darkness,
there could be infinite moments
of light,
full of happiness
and laughter
and love.

Read Him Again

Every single time
I sit down
in my tattered black leather
lounge chair
feeling hopeless,
feeling desperate,
feeling like there's just
no point
to any of it,
I pour a glass of wine,
read
a couple pages of
Bukowski,
and it's then I realize,
my soul humming
along with his words,
that it's okay,
I can keep going,
everything
will be okay,
at least
for another day,
and then I'll just
read him again.

D. Michael Hardy

The Death Café

We'll sit around
and drink lattes
talking about Death
in all her horrid,
glorious forms
until the sun
comes up,
then go to bed
and dream
as if we're immortal,
destined
to never kiss
her cold, captivating lips
ourselves.

Thrive

And it seems
I am meant
to suffer
in this life
so that in some
small ways
my writing
might
thrive.

D. Michael Hardy

Move

Move slowly
    toward
        a better way of
            life,
      out of the old
          solitary shackles
       once constructed
          for yourself
    and into something
        new,
      something free
        and wild
      and brilliant
             and all your own.

So move.

Another Sad Poem

Someone once told me
I should write
happy poems,
love poems,
poems of joy
and passion
and tenderness,
but I just shook my head,
laughed and said,
"That's just not me, baby,"
and then I went to the bar,
got myself another drink
of whiskey,
wrote another sad poem,
smiling
with tears in my eyes
as pen scratched paper,
and I knew
this is how it was
always meant to be.

D. Michael Hardy

Playful Little Boy

I've watched you grow
from that playful little boy
who loved Blues Clues
and Batman,
Hot Wheels and Spiderman,
to a curious kid
who always wanted to play
with the adults,
who wanted to grow up
too fast
and skip the agony
of adolescence,
and now, into a young man
trying to find his way
in a world
too often ugly and cruel.

You've got a lot of opinions
on a great many things,
and though you may often
feel the pressures of others
who try to tell you
how wrong you are, or
how you're not good enough,
I'd like to reassure you,
if I can, that
those pressures will eventually pass,
but the truth is, kid,
it's all up to you

to decide what's important
and what's trivial,
to decide who you are,
who you want to be,
and who you'll become,
and the beauty of this life
is that you can change
your mind
in an instant.

Today, that playful little boy
is long gone,
that curious kid
merely a memory,
but the man you've become,
and are becoming
each day
makes me proud,
even if I don't always tell you,
or act like it,
because I know
you're going through a lot
and maybe often feel
alone in this world,
but as long as I'm around,
you'll never be alone,
and you'll always have family
who love and support you,
and your infinite dreams.

D. Michael Hardy

Gone, Too Soon

Two of you now,
no wait, three,
gone forever,
gone too soon,
before we could share
another drink, another laugh,
another conversation about music
or films
or politics
or books
or guns,
about our lives and hopes and dreams,
and I still remember
the scent of your living rooms,
of dogs and sweat and gun oil,
sweet perfume and pasta sauce,
cigarettes and chocolate,
the sounds of a clock ticking,
the whirring of a big box fan,
dogs at play,
and a little girl
humming in the background,
but now your seats at tables
are left vacant,
the spaces you once occupied
at parties are void
of your illustrious selves,
and all the rest of us
you've left behind

The Ghosts of Us

can do
is carry on,
with memories of you
tacked to our hearts
and minds
like post-its
we are forever reading.

D. Michael Hardy

Two Years Sober

The other day
on Facebook
an old friend posted,
"two years sober"
and at first I thought,
"why?"
but soon realized
he's getting older,
as am I,
and we need to take care
of ourselves,
and then I thought,
"good for you bud"
but then remembered
all those nights
he and I shared together,
drinking and laughing and bullshitting
about our lives
until the sun came up.

We haven't seen each other
in just about two years now,
and it makes me sad
to think that maybe
that's the reason why,
the reason
he keeps his distance,
and that maybe
there's no longer

room for me
in his new
sober life.

D. Michael Hardy

Haunted

We are forever
haunted
by ghosts
of regret,
those things
we wish we had
done, or done
differently
than we did,
but rather than
allow these ghosts
to keep us up
at night,
rattling their chains
and opening closet doors,
we must instead accept them
into our lives,
embrace them
as lessons learned,
so that we are no longer
haunted,
but gifted
by insight,
hard-won experience,
and the tears
shed along the way.

Familia Melancholia

There is a darkness
which coils like a snake
in my mind
at times,
and they say
it's hereditary,
and looking back
that certainly
seems true,
Fitzgerald suffered,
as did you,
although as a little boy
I failed to see it,
so well hidden
as it was
behind your warm smiles,
your soft-spoken words,
sweet as the honeysuckle
that grew wild
in your backyard.

Now, as an adult,
I can recall that darkness,
the hints of despair
clouding your eyes,
the sullen silences
as we swayed together
on that old porch swing
and watched traffic flow by,

D. Michael Hardy

and later came stories
of melancholia,
of multiple suicide attempts
and days spent languishing
in bed, of your wailing
in the dead of night,
crying out for a sister
tragically lost
long ago.

But to that little boy
you knew,
you were the matriarch,
the one everyone else
gathered around
for stories
of the old days,
for comfort
and a sense of belonging,
for every holiday
and family reunion,
and it took a long time
to understand
those dark moods of mine
had been yours too,
the strength
it must have taken
to smile through
such overwhelming despair
and laugh
along with the rest of us,
and how lonely
it must have felt
to keep on going,
when all you really wanted

was to disappear.

If only
I could tell you
now,
how much more
I admire you,
love you,
and respect you
for sticking around
for as long
as you did.

D. Michael Hardy

Final Words

There were so many
moments
I wondered
what I'd say
to you
if I ever saw you
again.

I just never
expected
those words
to be spoken
at your funeral.

Nothing

There is nothing
wrong
with doing nothing,
with merely existing
in the unproductive moment.

Often, it is the best
therapy
for everything
else.

So take a moment
and do
nothing.

D. Michael Hardy

A Morning at Home

I've yet to sleep,
the garbage men
have come and gone,
the house
is 64 degrees
and illuminated by candles
still burning,
the moon bright,
almost full,
books everywhere,
words
spinning in my head,
the whiskey
is plentiful,
cats scampering
from room to room,
and the music plays on.

Reminisce

Tonight, it became real
as I sat
in your living room
on that old, tattered couch
where we'd carried on
countless conversations
over the years,
and I kept expecting
you
to emerge from the back room
with that smug grin
spread across your face and say,
"gotcha motherfucker,"
all smiles and cocksure,
and all of this would be
over,
a bad dream,
a bad joke you thought
I'd get a kick out of,
but you never did,
because you really are
gone,
a ghost,
no longer here
to shake hands with
as I come through the door,
to hold back that little pup
that at one time
wanted to eat me alive,

D. Michael Hardy

only later to lick me to death,
to bullshit about girls
and guns and cars
and what the hell
we're doing
with our lives,
about your dream
of a house
with a garage the size
of Montana,
and tonight
I've finally
had to acknowledge this
as I sat around
with your family,
the only one there
not bound by blood,
even though
you were a brother
in every other conceivable way.

But this isn't easy,
you know,
and I wish
I could just talk to you
about all of this,
laugh like we used to,
even if it would be
our final conversation,
our final good night,
but that's usually
how things go, isn't it?
We leave so much
unsaid

because we always think
there'll be "another time"
when the truth is,
nothing is guaranteed.

But tonight,
I found myself
sitting on that same couch,
feeling your presence
in the room
as I spoke to your sister,
your kids and your new wife,
now a widow,
and I think all of us
on some level just knew
you were there with us,
smiling
with a glint
of tears in your eyes
as you listened
to us reminisce
of our once
wild adventures
we all shared with you.

Rest in peace, brother.

D. Michael Hardy

What I'll Miss

I often wonder
what I'll miss
after I leave
this old house,
when I can no longer
cross this familiar threshold
and smile
at the subtle scratches
in the wooden balusters
where my cats
often sit, gazing
out the screen door
transfixed
by the magnificence
of the world outside,
when I'll no longer
hear the click-clacking
of that old ceiling fan
above my bed
as if the damned thing
might just spin off
at any moment
and slice me in two,
when the memories
of old friends
drunk at parties, crying
on my shoulder, sharing
a drink or a meal or a laugh
rush back like old

The Ghosts of Us

movies playing silently
on my eyelids,
when it's the only place
in this great big world that
feels, truly, like home.
I often wonder
what I'll miss
after I leave
this old house,
and often wonder
if this old house
will miss me too.

D. Michael Hardy

Respite

I surround myself
with books
because the outside
world
is often too much
for me,
and they bring me
comfort
more than most anything
else,
these little treasures
of paper, ink, and glue,
their words are worlds,
transporting and timeless,
a respite
from the terror
of everyday life,
the fatal futility
of personal perfection.

Final Conversation

I barely remember
our final conversation,
only that it was casual,
as if Death
wasn't soon expected,
and we'd made plans
to get together
the following week,
only the following week
you were gone,
and I was left
trying to remember
the words
of our final conversation.

D. Michael Hardy

Holding On to the Past

The things which
haunt us most
are the ghosts
we choose to
keep.

And so
we must choose
who
to hold on to,
and when
to let go.

Almost Tomorrow

The sun's coming up
and it's almost tomorrow.

And what will we do
with another tomorrow?

Make promises
we can't keep?

Plans
we'll be late
executing?

Goals
we'll fail
to achieve?

So much rests
on the possibility
of tomorrow.

We continuously
put off today
what can be done tomorrow.

But there's no guarantee
we'll be here,
no one to assure us
we have another day,

D. Michael Hardy

another twenty-four hours
to do all those things
we've promised ourselves
we'd get to,
all those things
we promised others
we'd do for them.

I sit outside
drinking, listening
to the rain,
to a neighbor's dog
barking,
and tell myself
I'll take my parents
to the pound
to look for that dog
they keep wishing for.

And then tomorrow comes,
and we don't go to the pound.

Tomorrow is a fantasy
just out of reach,
never a guarantee.

Don't keep planning
for tomorrow,
because today
just might be
the last day
we'll get
to see.

Smoke

When it began,
I never figured
anyone
would ever read
the words I wrote,
they were like
smoke
from a cigarette,
drifting through
my fingers
and onto the page,
the ashes became
the sentences
and dialogue
of characters
that would carry me through
the darkest of days,
providing comfort
when nothing else could,
not even
the soothing numbness
alcohol provided,
or the warm embrace
of another human being,
and now
this smoke is thicker,
darker,
like that of a
bonfire

D. Michael Hardy

burning deep within me,
drifting farther out,
signaling
to others,
to the world,
that I am coming,
that I will be
with them
soon.

Ghost

And when I become
a ghost,
that which exists
where dust and regret
linger,
look for me
only
in the places
I've been,
think of me
fondly
and without regret,
dream of me
softly
in those silent hours
before dawn,
speak of me
often
so that some part of me
might live on,
and make my funeral
one party
you'll never
forget.

Acknowledgements

First, I'd like to thank everyone who has come into my life and inspired me to write poetry, whether you knew it or not. None of this would exist without you. Thank you to those who have supported my writing over the years, I truly appreciate you. Thanks to my parents for always supporting my dreams. And thank you Ioulia Svyatogor, for helping me shape this book to be what it is, and for everything else.

D. Michael Hardy is a writer of fiction and poetry. He currently studies creative writing at Southern New Hampshire University and is the author of *Pain & Longing: Poetry and Photography*. He lives in Tampa, Florida.

You can find him at www.dmichaelhardyauthor.com

www.ingramcontent.com/pod-product-compliance
Lightning Source LLC
LaVergne TN
LVHW041221080426
835508LV00011B/1031